The Sex Education Dictionary

## Also in this series

***My Changing Body***
*Girl's Edition*

***My Changing Body***
*Boy's Edition*

# The
# Sex Education
# Dictionary

## The A's through the Z's of the Birds and the Bees

## Linda Picone

Fairview Press
Minneapolis

Published by Fairview Press, 2450 Riverside Avenue, Minneapolis, Minnesota 55454. Fairview Press is a division of Fairview Health Services, a community-focused health system, affiliated with the University of Minnesota, providing a complete range of services, from the prevention of illness and injury to care for the most complex medical conditions. For a free current catalog of Fairview Press titles, please call toll-free 1-800-544-8207. Or visit our Web site at www .fairviewpress.org.

Library of Congress Cataloging-in-Publication Data
Picone, Linda.
  The sex education dictionary : by Linda Picone.
    p. cm.
  ISBN 978-1-57749-231-3 (alk. paper)
  1. Sex—Dictionaries. 2. Human reproduction—Dictionaries. I. Title.
HQ35.P53 2010
613.9083'03—dc22
                                        2010005782

Printed in Canada
First Printing: August 2010

14  13  12  11  10      7  6  5  4  3  2  1

Based on a book by Dr. Dean Hoch and Nancy Hoch, MS
Book design by Ryan Scheife, Mayfly Design (www.mayflydesign.net)
Illustrations by Bruce A. Wilson (www.brucewilsonart.com)

Medical Disclaimer:
This publication is designed to provide accurate and authoritative information in regard to the subject matter covered. It is sold with the understanding that neither the author nor the publisher is engaged in the provision or practice of medical, nursing, or professional healthcare advice or services in any jurisdiction. If medical advice or other professional assistance is required, the services of a qualified and competent professional should be sought. Neither Fairview Press nor the author is responsible or liable, directly or indirectly, for any form of damages whatsoever resulting from the use (or misuse) of information contained in or implied by these documents.

# Contents

# Introduction

This is a book that doesn't tell a story. It's a collection of words and the descriptions of what they are — and they're all part of *your* story, the story of a child becoming a young person and then an adult.

You know what's happening to your body and your feelings, but you may not know the right words to describe it. Or you may hear the words and wonder, "Just what does *that* mean?" We hope this book will help you find and learn the correct words for this important time in your life.

When you have questions, look for the answers in this book, but remember that your parents know a lot about growing up, too. They were kids once themselves!

And while you're at it, you can have a little fun with the games and puzzles at the back of the book. These may challenge you a bit, but they'll also help you be more comfortable with the words we use.

## Words You Can't Say in Front of Your Parents

The kinds of slang words or dirty words you hear at school or in movies aren't in this dictionary, because:

1. You should learn the real word for each body part, emotion, or action.
2. We want you to think about your body in a good way. Slang words often say ugly things about your body.
3. Slang words change all the time. They can mean one thing today and a different thing tomorrow. People may use one word in Texas and a completely different word in New Hampshire for exactly the same thing.

You may hear words you don't know and want to look up what they mean. Ask your parents, guardians, or a friend you trust for the real word so that you can read about it in this dictionary.

## For Parents and Guardians

You are your children's most important teachers. They learn from what you say and, even more important, from what you do. If you dodge their questions about how their bodies are changing and what it means, they get the message that it's something they're supposed to be embarrassed about. If you listen and try to help them understand their new physical and emotional selves, they learn something quite different: They're growing up and it may be kind of strange, but it's okay; everyone goes through it.

We encourage you to use this book as a tool to help in those conversations with your children. This dictionary provides accurate, science-based definitions of common and not-so-common terms. The games and puzzles are here to take away some of the discomfort with words we use to describe our bodies—and just to have fun.

No book can substitute for parental guidance on moral, religious, and philosophical values about relationships, sexuality, families, and what it means to be a person in our culture. Your children need to talk to *you*. We hope you'll use this dictionary as a way to start some of the important conversations you need to have with your children.

# Dictionary Terms:

# Definitions and Illustrations

**A**

**abdomen** (AB-doe-men). The middle part of your body. Inside your abdomen are the stomach, intestines, liver, bladder, kidneys, and other organs. In a female, the uterus also is in the abdomen.

**abortion** (a-BORE-shun). The removal of an unborn embryo from a woman's uterus. Today, the word "abortion" is usually used to describe a planned removal, but an abortion can happen naturally as well (spontaneous abortion). A planned abortion is usually done in a doctor's office or a hospital and does not produce a baby.

**abstinence** (AB-stih-nens). *Not* doing something (or abstaining). Some people practice abstinence from sexual intercourse as a way to prevent pregnancy.

**abusive relationship** (a-BYOO-siv ree-LAY-shun-ship). When one person in a relationship hurts the other in some way, whether physically, such as hitting, or with ugly words and actions.

**acne** (ACK-nee). Bumps on the skin caused by changing hormones. Acne can be mild or severe with just a few small, reddish bumps or with many large bumps that can ooze pus. Keeping the skin clean, avoiding picking at the face, and medication can help. See a doctor for serious acne. Also called pimples or zits.

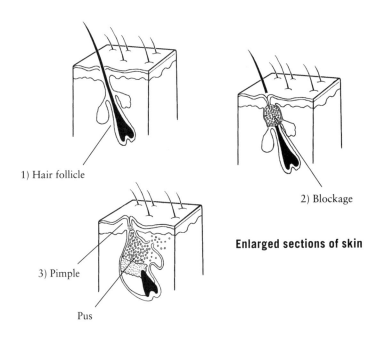

1) Hair follicle

2) Blockage

**Enlarged sections of skin**

3) Pimple

Pus

**acquaintance rape** (uh-QUAYNT-ens rape). When sex is forced by someone who knows or has met the victim. Also called date rape.

**acquired immunodeficiency syndrome** (uh-QUI-urd im-YOU-no-de-FISH-en-see sin-drome) or **AIDS.** A viral disease that causes the immune system to fail. It can be spread through sex, blood, needles, or from an infected mother to her unborn baby, but not from casual contact like shaking hands. Although AIDS cannot be cured, and can lead to death, there are treatments today that can help people with AIDS live for many years.

**Adam's apple.** The bump on a boy's or man's throat caused by the larynx. The Adam's apple gets bigger as a boy becomes a man. Girls have them, too, but usually they are small. This part of the throat is where the vocal cords are.

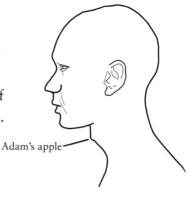

Adam's apple

**adolescence** (add-oh-LESS-ens). The time of life when a girl begins changing into a young woman and a boy changes into a young man. Adolescence usually starts sometime between the ages of eight and thirteen and can last for years. People go through adolescence in different ways, usually depending on what adolescence was like for their parents. *See also* puberty.

**adoption** (uh-DOP-shun). Legally adding a child to your family who was not born into it. An adult or adults may choose to adopt a child whose parents they don't know, or may adopt the child of a friend or family member (a grandparent may adopt a grandchild, if the child's parents can't take care of it, for example). Adoption means the parents will raise the child and be responsible for it, as if that child were born to them.

**adultery** (uh-DULL-tuh-ree). Sexual intercourse between a married person and someone other than her or his husband or wife.

**affection** (uh-FECK-shun). Having warm feelings for something or someone.

**afterbirth.** The placenta, a temporary organ, provides a developing baby with food and oxygen during pregnancy. Shortly after the baby is born, the placenta is expelled from the mother. This is called the afterbirth.

**AIDS.** *See* acquired immunodeficiency syndrome.

**amenorrhea** (a-MEN-uh-REE-uh). Absence of menstruation. The primary form is when a female, age sixteen or older, has not had her first menstrual period. The secondary form is when a female's menstruation cycle ceases. In both cases, the female should see a physician about possible problems with her reproductive system.

**amniocentesis** (AM-nee-oh-sen-TEE-sis). A medical test that can be done during pregnancy to determine the sex of the unborn child, check on lung development, or see whether the baby may have a genetic disorder. During the procedure, a doctor inserts a hollow needle through the abdomen and into the uterus of the pregnant woman and withdraws a sample of amniotic fluid.

**amnion** (AM-nee-ahn). The inner layer of tissue of the amniotic sac.

**amniotic fluid** (am-nee-AH-tik fluid). The fluid surrounding an unborn child inside the mother's uterus.

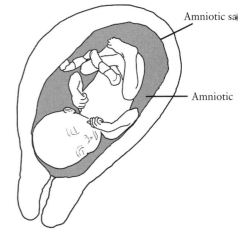

Amniotic sa

Amniotic

**amniotic sac** (am-nee-AH-tik sac). A thin membrane that forms a closed sac around the fetus inside the mother's uterus. It contains the amniotic fluid.

**anal intercourse** (A-nul IN-ter-kors) **or anal sex** (A-nul seks). The insertion of a man's penis into the anus of another person for sexual stimulation.

**anorexia nervosa** (ann-a-REX-ee-uh ner-VOS-uh). An eating disorder in which a person becomes obsessed with losing weight and engages in dangerous behavior, such as starvation; use of pills, laxatives, or diuretics; and obsessive calorie counting and exercise. Anorexia nervosa can cause long-term damage to your body and, if not treated, can lead to serious illness and even death.

**antibody** (AN-tih-body). A protein your blood makes to fight toxins (poisons) or foreign organisms in your body, such as bacteria or viruses. In many cases, antibodies can neutralize toxins and help eliminate infections. When a person has AIDS or another disease of the immune system, the body doesn't make antibodies in the same way and can't fight disease.

**anus** (A-nus). The opening in the body through which bowel movements pass.

**areolae** (ah-REE-oh-lay). On a woman's breasts, the area of darkened skin surrounding the nipples. The singular form is areola.

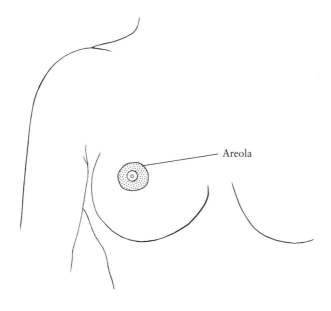

Areola

**arousal** (uh-ROU-zal). Feelings of strong physical attraction toward another person; sexual excitement. Male and female bodies have different reactions to being aroused.

**arranged marriage**. In some cultures, families or others choose the husbands or wives for their children. The two getting married may not meet until their wedding day, or close to it.

**artificial insemination** (ar-tih-FISH-ul in-sem-ih-NAY-shun). A medical procedure in which semen is placed into the vagina using a syringe. The semen may come from the woman's partner or from another man. Artificial insemination is used to help a woman get pregnant when attempts to conceive through intercourse have failed.

**B**

**baby.** A newborn child.

**baby blues.** *See* postpartum depression.

**Bartholin's glands** (BAR-tuh-linz glandz). Two small glands in the vagina that secrete a fluid that lubricates the vagina when a female is sexually aroused.

**basal body temperature.** Your body temperature when you first wake up. A woman can keep track of her daily basal body temperature to help her determine when she is ovulating.

**belly button.** *See* navel.

**binge eating** (binj eating). An eating disorder in which a person frequently and compulsively eats an unusually large amount of food in a short period of time. Someone with this disorder may binge two or more times a week. This behavior can cause serious health problems, including obesity and high blood pressure. Some people binge and then force themselves to throw up (binge and purge), which is also very dangerous. *See also* bulimia nervosa; compulsive overeating.

**birth.** The process that brings a baby into the world. After forty weeks, or about nine months, in the uterus, a baby is ready to be born. Normally, the baby comes through the birth canal, or vagina, but babies also may be delivered by Cesarean section through a small cut in the abdomen.

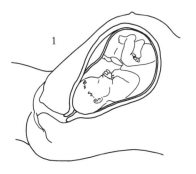

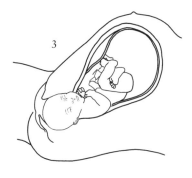

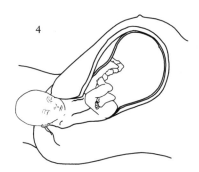

**birth canal.** The vagina is sometimes called the birth canal because a baby travels through it from the uterus when it is being born.

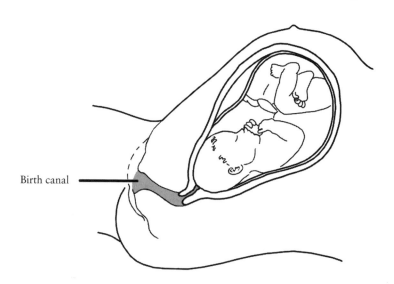

Birth canal

**birth control** or **contraception** (con-tra-SEP-shun). Any method used to prevent a baby from being conceived.

**birth control pills.** Pills taken by a woman to prevent pregnancy. They contain hormones that either prevent ovulation, thicken cervical mucus to prevent sperm from reaching an egg, or both. Also called "the pill."

**birth control shot.** *See* contraceptive injection.

**birth disorder** or **birth defect.** An abnormality of structure, function, or body metabolism that is present at birth. It may be minor or serious, and may be caused by genetic, environmental, or unknown factors.

**bisexual** (by-SEKS-you-uhl). A person who is sexually attracted to both sexes, male and female.

**bladder.** The organ in the body where urine is stored.

**blastocyst** (BLAST-oh-sist). The third stage in the development of a baby inside the mother's body. This stage starts about five days after the sperm fertilizes the ovum (egg), and continues until about the fourteenth day. During this stage, the fertilized ovum travels through the Fallopian tube to the uterus and attaches (implants) itself to the uterine wall, called the endometrium.

**body fluids.** Any fluids that exist normally in the body, such as blood, semen, sweat, and vaginal secretions.

**body image.** The way a person sees his or her own body. During puberty and adolescence, young people are often uncomfortable with all the changes their bodies are going through and may start to see themselves as unattractive or clumsy—whether they are or not. If a poor body image isn't dealt with in a healthy way, it can lead to problems such as low self-esteem, eating disorders, and depression.

**body odor.** Odor created by perspiration combined with natural bacteria on the skin. It may begin to be noticeable during puberty, when sweat glands become more active. Bathing daily with soap and water—and using deodorant if needed—usually prevents the odor.

**bosom** (BUHZ-em). A woman's breasts or a man's chest.

**Bradley method.** A method of natural childbirth developed by Dr. Robert Bradley. The method emphasizes abdominal breathing techniques designed to help a mother relax during childbirth.

**Braxton Hicks contractions.** *See* false labor.

**B**

**breast self-examination (BSE).** A technique developed to help a woman check herself for lumps or changes in her breasts. Women do breast self-examinations to find any change that might be a sign of breast cancer. When breast cancer is found and treated early, women have a better chance of overcoming it.

**breastfeeding.** After a baby is born, hormones cause the mother's breasts to make milk. In breastfeeding, the baby sucks milk from the mother's breasts for nourishment. Also called nursing.

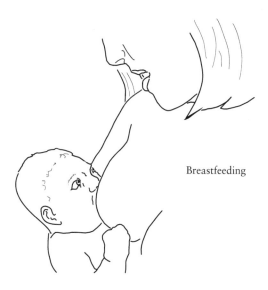

Breastfeeding

**breasts.** Two glands on a female's chest that begin to develop and grow during puberty, sometime between ages eight and thirteen. Their primary purpose is to provide nourishment to a woman's baby. A mother's milk develops in her breasts soon after her child is born. Breasts can also be important during sex. Many women are aroused when their breasts are touched, and men may become aroused when looking at or touching a woman's breasts. Also called mammary glands.

**breech birth.** When a baby comes through the birth canal buttocks or feet first, rather than head first as in a normal birth. This can be dangerous for both the mother and the baby. Therefore, the doctor or midwife will try to reposition the baby so the head will come out first. If that isn't possible, the baby may be delivered by Cesarean section.

**bulbourethral glands** (bul-boe-you-REE-thrul glandz). *See* Cowper's glands.

**bulimia nervosa** (buh-LEE-mee-uh ner-VOS-uh). An eating disorder in which a person engages in binge eating and then purges to prevent weight gain. The purging can be done in a variety of ways, including self-induced vomiting and abuse of diuretics or laxatives. Bulimia can lead to serious health problems.

**buttocks** (buht-ocks). The rump or rear end; the part of the body a person sits on.

**calendar method** or **rhythm method.** A fertility awareness method of birth control in which a woman keeps track of the dates of her menstrual cycles and only has sexual intercourse when she is not as likely to get pregnant. *See also* fertility awareness method.

**celibate** (SELL-ih-but). Someone who doesn't have sexual intercourse.

**cell.** A tiny, microscopic piece of matter capable of interacting with other cells to perform the functions of life.

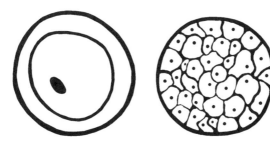

Single cell            Group (division) of cells

**cell division.** The way cells multiply, by dividing. Cell division is the way a new baby is formed in the body of the mother. *See also* egg cell.

**cervical cap** (SER-vih-kuhl cap). A barrier method of contraception in which a small, plastic cap fits snugly over the cervix to block sperm from entering.

C

**cervical mucus** (SER-vih-kuhl MYOO-kus). A sticky substance surrounding the opening of the cervix or neck of the womb.

**cervical os** (SER-vih-kuhl ohs). The opening of the cervix.

**cervix** (SER-vix). The narrow opening or neck of the uterus. It expands to allow a baby to be born.

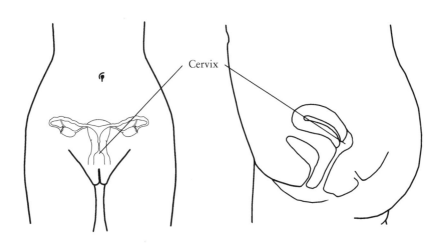

Frontal view                                    Side view

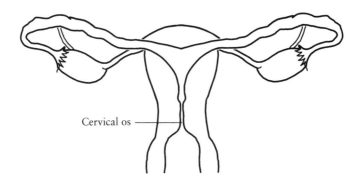

**Cesarean section** (sez-AIR-ee-an section) or **C-section.** An operation to deliver a baby by making a cut through the mother's abdomen. A C-section is done when a baby is not able to be born through the mother's vagina or birth canal.

**chancre** (SHANK-er). A small sore or ulcer; can be a symptom of syphilis.

**change of life.** *See* menopause.

**chaste** (chased). Being modest, pure, or innocent, or not having sexual relations before marriage.

**chlamydia** (kla-MIH-dee-ah). A bacterial infection that causes nongonococcal urethritis, a common sexually transmitted disease. In women, it is a leading cause of damage to the Fallopian tubes and inability to get pregnant.

**chorion** (KOR-ee-ahn). The outer layer of tissue of the amniotic sac.

**chorionic villi sampling** (KOR-ee-ahn-ick VILL-ee samp-ling) or **CVS.** A medical procedure in which a doctor inserts a thin tube into a pregnant female's vagina, through her cervix, and into her uterus to take a sample of the outer layer of the amniotic sac (called the chorion). The sample can help determine whether the developing fetus has any birth defects. This test can be done as early as the second month of pregnancy.

**chromosome** (CROME-a-zome). Part of a cell nucleus containing the genes that make up an individual.

C

**circumcision** (sir-kum-SIH-shun). The removal of the foreskin from a baby's penis. A doctor performs this operation a few days after a boy is born. Not all parents have this operation performed. Circumcision is a religious custom in the Jewish and Muslim faiths. It is also performed for health reasons, but many doctors now say it is not necessary.

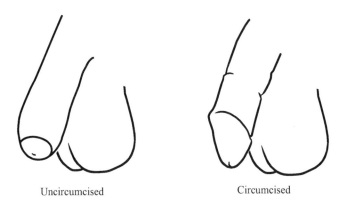

Uncircumcised                     Circumcised

**climax** (CLY-max). *See* orgasm.

**clitoral hood** (KLIT-eh-rull hood) or **prepuce** (PRE-pyoos). A fold of skin covering the clitoris. (In men, the prepuce refers to the foreskin covering the penis.)

**clitoris** (KLIT-eh-res). A small but sensitive part of a woman's sexual organs, located in the vulva above the vaginal opening. Its sexual function is similar to that of the male penis.

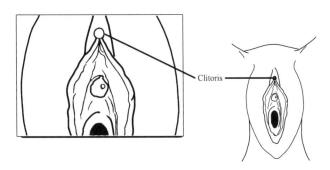

Clitoris

**coitus** (ko-EE-tus). *See* intercourse.

**coitus interruptus** (ko-EE-tus in-ter-UP-tus). When a male withdraws his penis from a woman's vagina just before ejaculation, to try to prevent pregnancy. This is not an effective pregnancy prevention method, since some sperm may enter the vagina even before ejaculation. Also called the pullout method or withdrawal.

**colostrum** (koh-LOSS-trum). A substance produced by a mother's breasts shortly after a baby is born. It is healthy for the newborn baby to drink the colostrum before the mother's milk "comes in," which usually happens a few days after birth.

**compulsive exercising.** A disorder in which a person exercises so much that it interferes with other obligations or activities and becomes unhealthy. Excessive exercise often begins as a way for someone to feel more in control of his or her body and weight. This behavior sometimes accompanies an eating disorder and can lead to serious health problems, including dehydration, stress fractures, reproductive problems, and heart problems.

**compulsive overeating.** An eating disorder in which a person consistently eats large amounts of food and uses food to cope with sadness, stress, and other emotions. Compulsive overeating can lead to health problems such as obesity, heart attack, high blood pressure, and high cholesterol.

**conceive** (con-SEEV). To become pregnant.

**conception** (con-SEP-shun). The coming together of an egg cell from the mother and a sperm cell from the father. This is the beginning of the development of a new baby.

Conception

C

**condom** (CON-dum). A soft rubber device that fits over a man's penis. It is worn during intercourse to prevent pregnancy and sexually transmitted diseases. Sometimes called a "rubber."

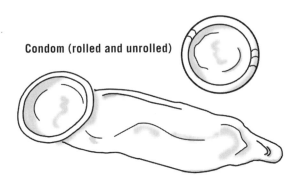

Condom (rolled and unrolled)

**congenital** (con-JEN-ih-tuhl). A condition existing at birth or acquired during development in the uterus; not an inherited trait or condition.

**conjoined twins.** Twins that are physically connected to one another at birth. This happens when the zygote of identical twins fails to separate completely. Conjoined twins can be connected almost anywhere, including at the head or abdomen. If they share organs, it can be difficult to separate them through surgery. Sometimes called Siamese twins.

**contraception** (con-tra-SEP-shun). *See* birth control.

**contraceptive** (con-tra-SEP-tiv). Any of a number of methods used to prevent pregnancy, such as the intrauterine device, condom, diaphragm, birth control pills, vasectomy, and tubal ligation.

**contraceptive foam** (con-tra-SEP-tiv fome). A contraceptive that a woman places in her vagina using an applicator. The foam kills sperm and keeps them from reaching the woman's egg.

**contraceptive implant** (con-tra-SEP-tiv IM-plant). A contraceptive that is surgically inserted into a woman's upper arm. It releases a synthetic form of progesterone into the woman's system to prevent ovulation, thereby preventing pregnancy. A contraceptive implant can prevent pregnancy for as long as three years.

**contraceptive injection** (con-tra-SEP-tiv in-JECK-shun). A hormone injection a woman gets to prevent pregnancy. The injection, which is effective for three months, contains progesterone. It prevents pregnancy by preventing ovulation. Also referred to as the "birth control shot."

**contraceptive patch** (con-tra-SEP-tiv patch). An adhesive patch that releases synthetic estrogen and progestin hormones into the system when placed on a woman's skin. It prevents pregnancy primarily by preventing ovulation. Ortho Evra® is a brand name for this type of contraceptive, commonly referred to as "the patch."

**contraceptive ring** (con-tra-SEP-tiv ring). A flexible, plastic ring that is placed in the vagina to prevent pregnancy. This contraceptive works by releasing hormones that prevent ovulation.

**contraceptive sponge** (con-tra-SEP-tiv sponj). A soft, plastic birth control device containing sperm-killing chemicals. A woman places the sponge in her vagina before intercourse to prevent pregnancy.

**contractions** (con-TRACK-shuns). The workings of the muscles of the mother's uterus that get stronger and stronger during labor, just before a baby is born. Contractions push a baby into the world. Also called uterine contractions.

**copulation** (cop-you-LAY-shun). Another name for sexual intercourse.

**corona** (kuh-ROW-nuh). The flared ridge at the back of the glans of the penis.

**couvade syndrome** (koo-VAHD sin-drome). A phenomenon in which the father of a pregnant woman's baby feels some of the same symptoms the woman feels. He may experience nausea, vomiting, bloating, and food cravings. This is also referred to as sympathetic pregnancy.

**Cowper's glands** (KOW-pers glandz). Two small, round glands located underneath a male's prostate gland. When a male is sexually aroused, the glands produce a fluid that lubricates the penis and protects the sperm as it travels through the acidic environment of the urethra. The formal term for these glands is bulbourethral glands.

**crab lice** or **crabs.** Insects that get into the pubic hair and cause severe itching and, in some cases, slight bleeding. Crab lice can be passed from one person to another through genital contact, or by using towels, bedding, or other materials that have been used by an infected person. Also called pubic lice.

**C-section.** *See* Cesarean section.

D

**date rape.** *See* acquaintance rape.

**date rape drug.** A chemical that makes a person unable to know what is happening or remember what has happened. Because the drug is difficult to see or taste, it can be put into a drink without the person's knowledge. This prevents the victim from resisting or remembering sexual activity.

**dating.** When two people who have romantic feelings for one another spend time together regularly.

**deoxyribonucleic acid** (dee-OX-ee-RYE-bo-new-CLEE-ik acid) or **DNA.** A chemical in the body that is a basic component of genes. DNA determines what characteristics a baby will inherit from its parents and is sometimes called the "blueprint of life."

**diabetes** (DIE-uh-BEE-teez). A disease that causes high levels of glucose or sugar in the blood. Diabetes can lead to problems with the heart, eyes, hearing, and circulation. Some people are born with diabetes, but many develop it as adults (or earlier). Women may have a form of diabetes, gestational diabetes, during pregnancy. Diet is very important in preventing and controlling diabetes.

D

**diaphragm** (DYE-a-fram). A rubber or plastic device a woman can insert into the vagina and over her cervix to prevent pregnancy. The diaphragm keeps sperm from getting to an egg cell.

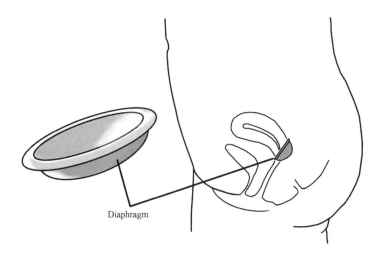

Diaphragm

**differentiation** (diff-ur-en-she-A-shun). The complicated process used by the cells to develop the different body parts of a baby in the uterus.

**dilation** (die-LAY-shun). The opening of the cervix in order to allow a baby to be born. The cervix dilates from zero to ten centimeters. At ten, it is completely open.

**discharge** (DIS-charj). A liquid that comes out of some part of the body. Vaginal discharge, for example, cleans and moistens the vagina and then leaves the body. When you have a cold, you may have nasal (from your nose) discharge.

**DNA.** *See* deoxyribonucleic acid.

**dominant trait** (DOM-in-ant trait). An inherited trait that over-rides another inherited trait. For example, brown eyes are dominant over blue eyes, meaning that if one parent contributes a gene for brown eyes and the other parent contributes a gene for blue eyes, the baby will have brown eyes.

D

**douche** (DOOSH). A current of water, or a commercial solution used to cleanse a body cavity—usually the vagina. Most experts say that it is not necessary to use anything to cleanse the vagina. Mild soap and water can be used on the external vaginal area—but not inside the vagina.

**drug overdose.** Taking so much of a drug—legal or illegal—that it is harmful. People may overdose on prescription drugs, illegal drugs, or even common drugs like aspirin.

**due date.** The approximate date that the delivery of a baby will occur. The due date is usually estimated as about forty weeks after the start of a woman's last period, although a doctor may consider other things when coming up with a due date.

# E

**eating disorders.** Disorders in which a person becomes ill because of improper eating habits. The most common are anorexia nervosa (self-starvation) and bulimia nervosa (binge eating and purging). These disorders are more common in females than in males.

**ectopic pregnancy** (eck-TOP-ik pregnancy). The abnormal implantation of a fertilized ovum outside the mother's uterus, such as in a Fallopian tube. *See also* tubal pregnancy.

**effacement** (eh-FACE-ment). The shortening or thinning of the cervix while a woman is preparing to give birth. As she's ready to have a baby, her cervix opens (dilates) and becomes shorter (effaces) so that the baby can come through the vagina and out into the world.

**egg cell.** The female reproductive cell. When an egg cell meets with a sperm cell in the female's body during intercourse, a baby may be conceived. Also called the ovum.

**ejaculation** (ee-JACK-you-lay-shun). The spurting of semen or sperm from a man's penis, which usually occurs at the climax of sexual intercourse or with some other stimulation.

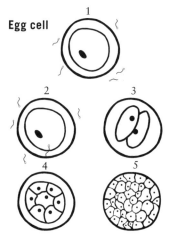

**Egg cell**

(1) Sperm reach the egg cell; (2) sperm cell enters the egg cell; (3) the cell divides, creating two cells, each of which divides. After a cell is created, it continues dividing (4, 5), making more and more cells in the process of forming a baby.

E

**ejaculatory ducts** (ee-JACK-yuh-la-tor-ee ducts). Canals in the male formed by the intersection of the vas deferens and the duct from the seminal vesicle. They pass through the prostate. Semen travels through them at the time of ejaculation.

**embryo** (EM-bree-oh). The fourth stage in the development of a baby inside the mother's body. This is the term for the development stage that starts about fourteen days after the sperm fertilizes the ovum (egg) and continues until the eighth week of pregnancy. After that, it is called a fetus.

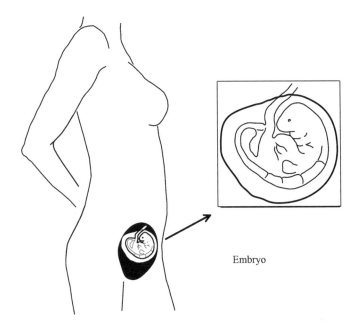

Embryo

**emergency contraceptive pill** (emergency con-tra-SEP-tiv pill). A pill a female can take after having sex to prevent pregnancy. The pill is effective when taken immediately after having sex or up to three to five days later. Also called "morning-after pill."

**emotions** (ee-MOE-shuns). Moods and feelings, ranging from extreme happiness to extreme sadness or anger. Emotions are strong and changeable in adolescence because of hormonal changes.

**endometrium** (en-doe-MEE-tree-um). The velvety lining of the uterus, where a fertilized egg develops.

E

**epididymis** (ep-ih-DID-ih-mus). Tiny tubes located behind each testicle, where sperm cells mature.

**epidural block** (ep-ih-DUR-al block). A form of anesthesia administered to the lower portion of the mother's body during childbirth to reduce pain.

**episiotomy** (ee-pee-zee-AH-tah-mee). A surgical incision a doctor may make in the mother from her vagina to the perineum at the time of birth. This is sometimes necessary to allow the baby to pass through the vagina more easily.

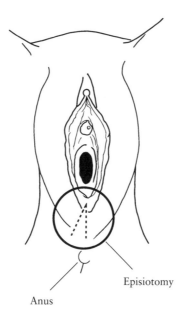

Episiotomy

Anus

**E**

**erectile dysfunction** (ee-RECK-tul dis-FUNK-shun) or **ED**. Not being able to have or keep an erection of the penis, making intercourse difficult. The cause may be physiological or psychological. Also called impotence.

**erectile dysfunction (ED) drugs.** Prescription drugs that help a man get and maintain an erection so that he can have sexual intercourse.

**erection** (ee-RECK-shun). The enlargement and hardening of a man's penis, which makes sexual intercourse possible. It is usually caused by sexual arousal, but sometimes it can be caused by other things as well.

**erotic** (ee-RAH-tic). Meant to or tending to arouse sexual desire or strongly affected by sexual desire.

**estrogen** (ESS-tro-jen). The female sex hormone produced in the ovaries. It affects the menstrual cycle and the development of a woman's sexual characteristics. Production of the hormone increases during puberty, resulting in the growth of breasts, development of pubic hair, and other changes.

**expulsion** (ex-PUL-shun). To force out. A fetus is sometimes expelled from the uterus, causing a miscarriage.

**Fallopian tubes** (fah-LOW-pee-an tubes). The part of a female's sex organs through which the egg cells pass from the ovaries to the uterus. The egg cell and sperm cell meet in a Fallopian tube when conception occurs. The fertilized egg cell then moves to the uterus. Also called oviducts.

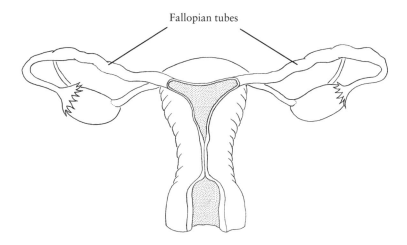

Fallopian tubes

**false labor.** Pains a pregnant woman may feel that are not real labor pains. Also called Braxton Hicks contractions.

**family planning.** The decisions parents make about how many children to have and when to have them.

**fantasize.** To daydream or think about things that you want to happen or that you would enjoy, including sexual things. People often fantasize while masturbating, as well as at other times.

**father.** The male partner who, with the mother, brings children into the world.

**female** (FEE-male). A girl or woman.

**female athletic syndrome** or **female athlete triad.** A phenomenon whereby a female who engages in extremely strenuous sports training develops three problems: eating disorders, amenorrhea (delay in first menstruation or interruption of normal menstrual cycles), and bone problems that can lead to early osteoporosis (brittle bones), or bone thinning and weakness.

**female condom** (FEE-male CON-dum). A barrier method of contraceptive in which a hollow tube with one closed end is put into the vagina. A male condom covers the outside of the penis, but the female condom covers the inside of the vagina. It prevents pregnancy and the transmission of disease.

**fertile** (FUR-till). Physically able to produce children.

**fertile mucus** (FUR-till MYOO-kus). A thick vaginal discharge that is released around the time the female ovulates. This mucus nourishes the male's sperm and allows it to pass freely through the female's cervix, thereby increasing the female's chances of getting pregnant.

**fertility** (fur-TILL-ih-tee). The state of being fertile.

**fertility awareness method.** Any method of birth control in which a woman carefully watches her body so that she has a good idea of when she is most and least likely to become pregnant. These signs include body temperature, vaginal secretions, and body changes before and during her period. A woman may use a fertility method to prevent pregnancy by not having intercourse when she is likely to be most fertile, or to increase the chance of becoming pregnant by having intercourse when she is most fertile. Fertility awareness is not considered a reliable way to avoid pregnancy, however. The calendar (or rhythm) method, the ovulation method, and the temperature method are different kinds of fertility awareness.

**fertilization** (fur-till-eye-ZAY-shun). The meeting of a sperm cell and an egg cell.

**Fertilization of an egg cell by a sperm cell**

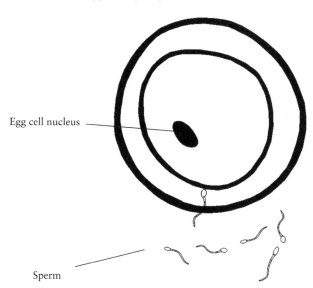

Egg cell nucleus

Sperm

**fetal alcohol syndrome** (FEE-tahl alcohol sin-drome). A serious, lifelong disorder in babies born to mothers who drink alcohol heavily while they are pregnant. It causes mental retardation and deformities.

**fetoscopy** (fee-TAH-scop-ee). Direct examination of the fetus using a fetoscope, which is a thin tube containing a scope.

**fetus** (FEE-tus). The fifth stage in the development of a baby inside the mother's body. This developmental stage starts in the eighth week of pregnancy and lasts until birth.

**fimbriae** (FIM-bree-ay). The fringe at the end of each Fallopian tube that help draw an egg cell into the tube on its way to the uterus.

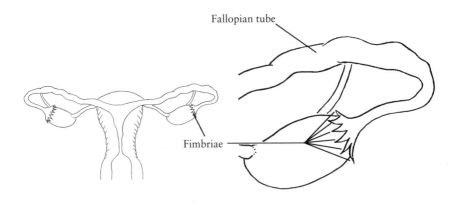

Fallopian tube

Fimbriae

**follicle** (FALL-ick-el). Small sac that contains egg cells in a female. Also refers to male sperm follicle.

**follicle-stimulating hormone** (FALL-ick-el STIM-you-late-ing HOR-moan) or **FSH**. A hormone produced by the pituitary gland in both males and females. FSH causes either the female egg follicle or the male sperm follicle to mature.

**fontanel** (fon-ton-ELL). The membrane-covered soft spot in a newborn baby's head, which closes a few weeks after birth.

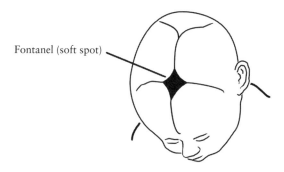

Fontanel (soft spot)

**food addiction** (food ah-DICK-shun). When food controls someone's behavior. Food addictions can include anorexia, or being afraid to eat; compulsive eating or binge eating, when someone can't stop eating; and other kinds of eating disorders.

**foreplay** (FOR-play). The kissing and touching that take place before intercourse. Foreplay helps both people become aroused.

**foreskin** (FOR-skin) or **prepuce** (PRE-pyoos). The skin covering the tip of the penis. This skin is removed when a boy is circumcised. (In women, the prepuce refers to the fold of skin covering the clitoris.)

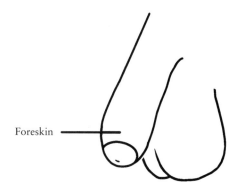

Foreskin

**formula** (FOR-myu-luh). Prepared liquid for babies, which can be used instead of or with breast milk. Formula can be made from cow's milk, soy milk, or certain nonmilk proteins. It's made to supply a baby with the nutrition it needs in the first year or two of life. Breast milk is the best nutrition for babies, but it's not always possible for mothers to breastfeed their babies.

**fornication** (for-nih-KAY-shun). Sexual relations between unmarried people.

**fraternal twins** (frah-TER-nal twinz). Two babies in one pregnancy, produced by two egg cells meeting with two sperm cells. Fraternal twins are siblings, but can look very different. Because they are created by two separate eggs and two separate sperm cells, they don't have the same genes. In fact, fraternal twins can be a boy and a girl. *See also* identical twins; twins.

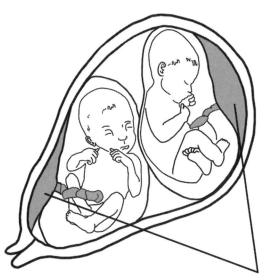

Fraternal twins (in the womb)
created from two separate eggs
and having separate placentas

**French kiss.** A romantic, passionate kiss in which the tongue enters the partner's mouth. Also referred to as a tongue kiss.

**frenulum** (FREN-ya-lum). The Y-shaped connecting tissue on the underside of the glans of the penis. It has many nerve endings and is very sensitive. Most of it is usually removed when a boy is circumcised.

F

gay. *See* homosexual.

gender (JEN-der). Sex; either male or female.

gender identity (JEN-der eye-DEN-tih-tee). A person's sense of being either a male or a female; the way you see yourself, whether it's male or female. A few people have a gender identity that is not the same as their physical gender. *See also* transgender.

genes (jeenz). The tiny units of heredity carried by the chromosomes.

genetic counseling. The application of what is known about human genetics to problems that have arisen or might arise during a pregnancy as a result of the parents' genetic makeup.

genetics (jen-ETT-icks). The science of heredity. How traits are passed by the genes from one generation to another.

genital herpes (JEN-ih-tal HER-peez). A type of viral, sexually transmitted disease that produces sores on the sex organs.

genital warts (JEN-ih-tal warts). A type of viral, sexually transmitted disease that produces small warts on and around the sex organs.

**genitalia** (JEN-in-TALE-ya) or **genitals** (JEN-ih-tals). The sex organs of a male or a female that can be seen easily.

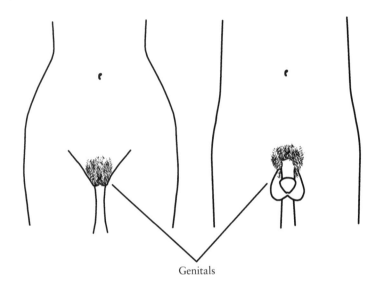

Genitals

**gestation** (jes-TAY-shun). The nine-month period during which a baby develops inside its mother's uterus.

**gestational diabetes** (jes-TAY-shun-uhl DIE-uh-BEE-teez). A type of diabetes that occurs only during pregnancy. Gestational diabetes leads to dangerously high blood sugar levels, which usually return to normal soon after the woman delivers her baby.

**glands.** Organs that make substances important in different parts of the body. The salivary glands, for example, make saliva that helps with eating and swallowing. Several glands make hormones that create the differences between male and female.

**glans** (glanz). In a male, the extreme end, or head, of the penis. In a female, the tip of the clitoris.

**gonococcus** (gone-oh-KAH-kus).
A kind of bacteria that causes
gonorrhea.

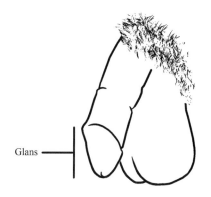

Glans

**gonorrhea** (gone-oh-REE-ah). A
common and serious sexually transmitted disease caused by bacteria
that can grow and multiply easily in
the warm, moist areas of the reproductive system in both men and
women.

**groin** (groyn). The part of the body where the legs join with the
torso, around the pubic area. Sometimes used to describe the area
where a male's sex organs are.

**growth spurt.** Refers to a period in a girl or boy's life when she or
he suddenly grows taller and begins to develop rapidly.

**gynecological exam** (guy-nah-co-LODGE-ih-kal exam). Examination by a doctor of a woman's vagina, cervix, and external
genitals.

**gynecologist** (guy-nah-CALL-oh-jist). A doctor who specializes in
all areas of female medicine.

**gynecology** (guy-nah-CALL-oh-gee). The kind of medicine that
deals with the diseases and hygiene of women.

**gynecomastia** (GUY-nah-kuh-MAS-tee-ah). Breast development in
men or boys. During adolescence, the breasts may be enlarged for
a while, but this usually goes away in two years or less.

**hemorrhoids** (HEM-or-oids). A mass of swollen, dilated veins near or inside the anal opening. Hemorrhoids are usually caused by straining to have a bowel movement. Hemorrhoids can also be caused by the pressure of pregnancy or the pushing a woman exerts when giving birth.

**hepatitis** (HEP-uh-tie-tus). A virus that attacks the liver. It occurs in different forms, designated by the letters A, B, C, D, and E, and can be transmitted through poor hygiene, sex, needles, or from an infected mother to her unborn baby. Some forms of the virus can be transmitted in other ways as well.

**heredity** (her-ED-ih-tee). The characteristics parents pass to their children through the genes.

**herpes** (HER-peez). Viral diseases of the skin. Some, but not all, are sexually transmitted. *See also* genital herpes.

**heterosexual** (het-er-oh-SEKS-you-uhl). A person who is sexually attracted only to people of the opposite sex. Also referred to as straight.

**homophobia** (hoe-moe-FOE-bee-ah). Fear of homosexuals and homosexuality.

**homosexual** (hoe-moe-SEKS-you-uhl). A person who is sexually attracted only to people of the same sex. Also referred to as gay.

**hormones** (HOR-moans). Chemicals secreted by the glands, some of which cause the sexual differences between men and women.

**human chorionic gonadotropin** (human KOR-ee-ahn-ick GO-nad-uh-TRO-pin) or **HCG.** A hormone produced during pregnancy. This is the hormone that is detected by pregnancy tests to determine whether a female is pregnant.

**human immunodeficiency virus** (human im-YOU-no-de-FISH-en-see virus) or **HIV.** A virus that can lead to acquired immunodeficiency syndrome (AIDS), which causes the immune system to fail. It can be transmitted through sex, needles, or from an infected mother to her unborn baby.

**human papillomavirus** (human pap-il-OH-ma-VI-rus) or **HPV.** A group of viruses that includes more than 100 different types. More than thirty of these viruses are sexually transmitted and can infect the genital area of men and women.

**human papillomavirus (HPV) vaccine** (human pap-il-OH-ma-VI-rus VAK-seen). Approved by the U.S. Food and Drug Administration in 2006, this vaccine, called Gardasil®, protects against four HPV types, which together cause 70 percent of cervical cancers and 90 percent of genital warts. It is approved for use in females ages nine to twenty-six. Studies are being done to determine whether the vaccine would also work for males.

**husband.** The male partner in a marriage.

**hygiene** (HIGH-jeen). Keeping the body parts clean and healthy.

**hymen** (HIGH-men). A layer of tissue (or membrane) covering or partially covering the opening of the vagina. It may be broken by intercourse, surgical incision, the use of tampons, or even strenuous exercise. Sometimes called by the old-fashioned term "maidenhead."

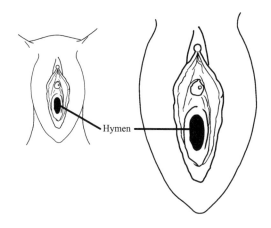

Hymen

**hysterectomy** (hist-er-ECK-tah-mee). An operation performed on a woman to remove her uterus. This may be necessary for a variety of different uterine problems. Without a uterus, a woman cannot bear children.

**identical twins** (eye-DEN-tic-al twinz). Two babies in one pregnancy, produced by one egg meeting with one sperm, but then dividing into two separate parts before developing as babies. Identical twins have the same genes and will look alike. *See also* fraternal twins; twins.

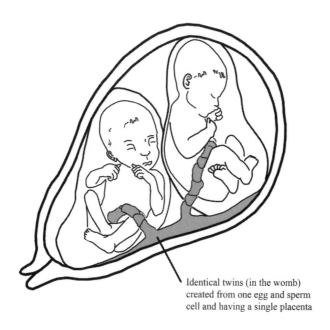

Identical twins (in the womb)
created from one egg and sperm
cell and having a single placenta

**immoral** (im-MORE-al). Going against what most people think is right. For some people, having sex before marriage, or with someone other than your husband or wife, is immoral.

**immune system.** The body's defense system against disease. When a person has AIDS, the immune system cannot combat infections.

**implantation** (im-plan-TAY-shun). The process in which a fertilized egg (one that has met with a sperm) attaches itself to the mother's uterine wall. There it develops into an embryo and then a fetus.

**Implantation**

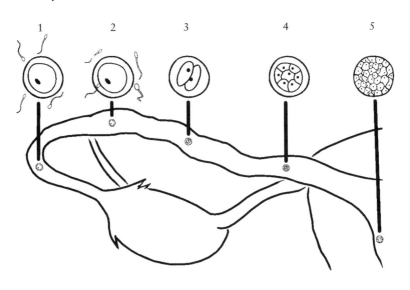

The fertilized egg (1) travels from the ovary through the Fallopian tube (2, 3, 4) until it reaches the uterus, where it attaches to the mother's uterine wall (5).

**impotence** (IM-pet-enz). *See* erectile dysfunction.

**in vitro fertilization** (in-VEE-tro fer-till-eye-ZAY-shun). Fertilization of an egg cell by a sperm cell outside a woman's body under laboratory conditions. The fertilized egg cell is then inserted into the uterus.

**incest** (IN-sest). Sexual intercourse between people who are so closely related they are forbidden by law to marry each other, such as a father and daughter or a brother and sister.

**infant.** A baby.

**infatuation** (in-FAT-u-ay-shun). A strong love or affection for another person that may not last long, or that is considered silly.

**infertility** (in-fer-TILL-i-tee). The inability to produce children. A man or a woman may be infertile.

**inguinal hernia** (ING-gwuh-nuhl HER-nee-uh). An organ pushing into a weak spot in the muscles of a male's lower abdomen, causing pain and a bulge in the scrotum. An operation is usually needed to repair the condition.

**inherited traits.** Features that parents pass on to their children, such as height, intelligence, eye color, type of hair, and skin color.

**intercourse** (IN-ter-kors) or **coitus** (KOH-ih-tus). The word "intercourse" can mean any interaction or communication, but in sexual terms it usually refers to the mating of a man and a woman. This involves the insertion of a man's penis into a woman's vagina and is called vaginal intercourse. During vaginal intercourse a baby may be, but is not always, conceived.

**intimate** (IN-tih-mit). Very personal or private. The term "intimate relations" sometimes refers to sexual relations between a man and a woman.

**intrauterine device** (in-tra-YOU-ter-in device) or **IUD**. A metal or plastic birth control device that a doctor can place in a woman's uterus through the vagina.

**jealous** (JEL-uhs). Being afraid of losing another person's love or affection.

**kinky** (KING-kee). Appealing to strange or unusual tastes, especially with regard to sexual matters.

**kiss.** To caress or touch with the lips to express affection.

**labia** (LAY-bee-eh). The folds of skin, or "lips," on the external female genitals surrounding the vaginal opening. There are an outer part (labia majora) and an inner part (labia minora).

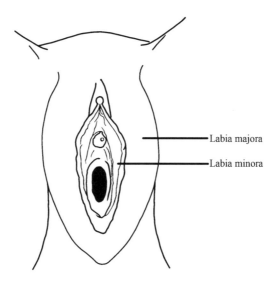

Labia majora
Labia minora

**labia majora** (LAY-bee-eh meh-JOR-eh). The outer lips surrounding the vaginal opening.

**labia minora** (LAY-bee-eh meh-NOR-eh). The inner lips surrounding the vaginal opening.

**labor.** The effort a mother puts forth during childbirth. When a woman is in labor, the uterus has contractions, which help push the baby out, and the cervix dilates (opens) to allow the baby to leave the uterus.

**lactational amenorrhea method** (lack-TAY-shun-al a-MEN-uh-REE-uh method). A method of birth control based on the idea that a woman who is nursing is less likely to ovulate for six months after a baby is born. It is not considered an effective way to prevent pregnancy.

**lactogenesis** (lack-toe-GEN-eh-sis). When milk production begins in a mother's breasts, shortly after birth.

**Lamaze** (lah-MAHZ). A method of childbirth involving the physical and psychological preparation of the mother. It helps reduce pain and often allows the mother to deliver the baby without the use of drugs.

**laparoscopy** (lap-ah-RAH-scop-ee). A procedure using a fiberoptic instrument that lets a doctor view the pelvic organs. Used mostly for diagnosing problems or for sterilization.

**larynx** (LAIR-inks). The organ in the throat where the vocal cords are. On boys or men, the larynx may bulge more on the outside and be called the Adam's apple.

**Leboyer method** (lah-BOY-er method). A natural childbirth method developed by Frederick Leboyer, M.D. The newborn baby is delivered in a quiet, dimly lit room and placed immediately on its mother's abdomen. Then the baby is placed in warm water and rocked gently.

L

**legal age.** The age when a person is allowed by the government to do certain things, such as drink alcohol, drive, or get married. For sexual relations, the legal age, or age of consent, is the age at which a person is considered old enough to understand and agree to being sexual. This age depends on where a person lives; in some states it's sixteen and in others it's eighteen.

**lesbian** (LEZ-bee-un). A female homosexual, or a woman who is attracted sexually only to other women.

**love.** The powerful emotional force that draws people together. Physical love between a man and a woman often results in the birth of a new human being.

**lubrication** (LOOB-ruh-KAY-shun). The act of producing or applying a wet, slippery substance to reduce friction and allow for smooth movements. When aroused, the female and male sex organs produce a lubricating mucus to allow the penis to easily enter the vagina during sex.

L

**lymphoceles** (LIMF-oh-seels). Firm, veinlike swellings on the penis, which can appear after injury or vigorous sexual stimulation, but also sometimes occur for no apparent reason. The swelling is caused by a blockage of the lymph glands near the corona and usually disappears in a few weeks without treatment.

**maidenhead.** Refers to the hymen. Also refers to the state of being a maiden or virgin. *See also* hymen.

**making out.** Sexual activity that doesn't include intercourse. Making out usually means kissing, hugging, and touching for the purpose of sexual pleasure. Also referred to as necking or petting.

**male.** A boy or man.

**mammary glands.** *See* breasts.

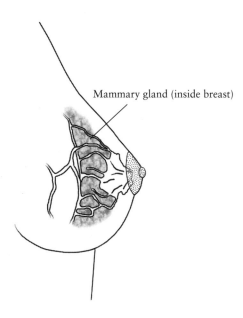

Mammary gland (inside breast)

M

**marriage** (MARE-ij). The legal joining of two people to declare that they are committed to each other and any children they may have.

**masturbate** (MASS-tur-bate). To stimulate your own sex organs, usually until you have a climax or orgasm.

**mate.** A spouse or close companion.

**maternal** (ma-TER-nal). Having to do with a mother.

**menarche** (MEN-ar-kee). A girl's first menstrual period.

**menopause** (MEN-oh-pahz). The time in a woman's life when the ovaries stop producing egg cells and hormones and menstruation ceases. Most women go into menopause in their early fifties, but it can be much earlier or later. It is sometimes called the "change of life."

**menstrual cramps** (MEN-stroo-al cramps). The painful feelings some females experience in their lower abdomens during their menstrual periods.

**menstrual cycle** (MEN-stroo-al cycle). The monthly fertility cycle most women experience, beginning with the first day of menstruation and continuing for about a month until the next cycle begins.

**menstrual period** (MEN-stroo-al period). Normally, the three- to six-day period when menstruation takes place. A girl can begin having menstrual periods as early as age eight, and usually no later than age sixteen. Also referred to as "period."

**menstruation** (MEN-stroo-AY-shun). The monthly discharge of blood from a female's uterus. Menstruation occurs approximately every twenty-eight days. If a baby is conceived, menstruation stops during the nine-month pregnancy period and then starts again after the baby is born.

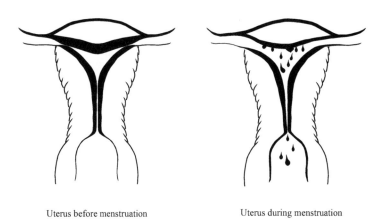

Uterus before menstruation          Uterus during menstruation

M

**midwife.** A health care professional—but not a doctor—who is trained to take care of a woman and her baby during pregnancy, childbirth, and the postpartum period.

**milk.** The nourishing liquid produced by a mother's breasts following the birth of a baby. A baby can live and grow for several months with nothing but its mother's milk.

**miscarriage** (MIS-care-ij). The loss of an embryo from the uterus, especially during the first three months of pregnancy.

**molest** (moh-LEST). To sexually abuse or harm someone, usually a child.

**molester** (moh-LESS-ter). Someone who sexually abuses or harms another person, usually a child.

**monogamy** (mah-NOG-ah-me). Marrying only once during a lifetime or having only one sexual partner at a time.

**mons pubis** (mons PYOO-bis) or **mons veneris** (mons VEN-ur-is). In females, the rounded, soft area above the pubic bone.

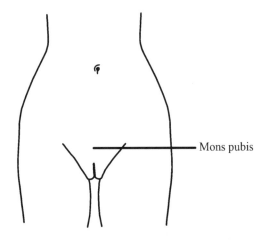

Mons pubis

**mood swings.** Emotional highs and lows that change quickly, such as going from being happy to feeling sad or angry. Changing hormones in adolescence can cause mood swings.

**morality** (more-AL-ih-tee). Living by high moral principles—sometimes refers to being chaste or not having sexual intercourse before marriage.

**morning sickness.** Nausea and vomiting experienced by many pregnant women, caused by the surge of hormones in the woman's body. Although a woman usually feels nauseous mostly in the morning during the first three months of pregnancy, it can happen at any time of day and can continue throughout the pregnancy.

**morning-after pill.** *See* emergency contraceptive pill.

**morula** (MOR-ya-lah). The second stage in the development of a baby inside the mother's body. This is the term for the development stage that starts about thirty hours after the sperm fertilizes the ovum (egg), and continues until about the fourth day.

**mother.** The female partner who, with a father, brings children into the world.

**mucus** (MYOO-kus). A sticky substance produced by various body parts, including a female's cervix and a male's Cowper's glands.

M

**mutual masturbation** (MYOO-chew-all mass-tur-BAY-shun). Sexual activity in which two people touch each other and come to orgasm, without sexual intercourse. Usually, people use their hands to give each other an orgasm.

**natural birth control** or **natural family planning.** *See* fertility awareness method.

**natural childbirth.** To give birth without having any kind of anesthesia to reduce pain and discomfort.

**nausea** (NAH-zee-ah or NAH-zha). Feeling sick to the stomach. *See also* morning sickness.

**navel** (NAY-vul). The depression in the middle of the abdomen that marks the point where the umbilical cord was attached. Also called the belly button.

**necking.** *See* making out.

**newborn.** A baby that has just been born.

**nipples.** The two small bumps on a male's chest and at the tips of a female's breasts. The nipple can be a sexually sensitive area for both the male and the female. For the breastfeeding mother, the nipple performs the same function as the nipple on a baby bottle: the baby sucks on the nipple to get the mother's milk.

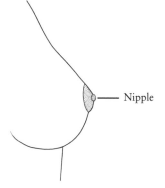

Nipple

**nocturnal emission** (nock-TURN-uhl ee-MISH-un). The release of sperm while sleeping. This happens occasionally, usually starting around age of thirteen. Also called a wet dream.

**nongonococcal urethritis** (nahn-gahn-uh-KAH-kul yer-eh-THRY-tus) or **NGU**. A sexually transmitted disease (not gonorrhea).

**noninsertive sex.** *See* outercourse.

**nonoxynol-9** (non-OX-i-nol-nine). A spermicide used in contraceptive products. Nonoxynol-9 may be in cream, foam, or jelly form. It does not reduce the risk of sexually transmitted diseases.

**nursing.** *See* breastfeeding.

N

# O

**obesity** (oh-BEE-sit-ee). Extreme overweight. Those who are obese can suffer from a number of health problems, including heart disease, diabetes, some kinds of cancer, and arthritis.

**obstetrician** (ob-sta-TRIH-shun). A doctor who takes care of a woman and her baby during pregnancy, childbirth, and right after birth.

**oral intercourse** (OR-ul IN-ter-kors) or **oral sex** (OR-ul seks). The placement of the mouth on the genitals of another person for sexual stimulation.

**orchidometer** (or-kih-DOM-uh-ter). An instrument used to measure the volume of testicles. Doctors monitor the size of testicles because abnormal size can be a sign of certain diseases or maturation problems.

**orgasm** (OR-gaz-um). The main moment of sexual pleasure, when the muscles contract and an overall intense good feeling happens. Males usually ejaculate when they have an orgasm. Orgasm usually happens after the sex organs have been stimulated through sexual contact of some kind, or through masturbation, but it's possible to climax even without the sexual organs being touched. Also called the climax.

**os** (ohs). The opening of the uterus.

**osteoporosis** (ah-stee-oh-por-OH-sis). A disease that causes bones to become fragile and more likely to break. A person who does not have enough calcium in his or her diet during puberty is more likely to develop this disease when he or she is older. Osteoporosis affects both sexes, but women are four times more likely to develop the disease.

**outercourse.** The sexual stimulation of a partner without having intercourse. Couples may engage in this type of sexual activity to prevent pregnancy and sexually transmitted disease. A couple may also choose to have outercourse if they don't feel ready to have intercourse. Also called noninsertive sex.

**ova** (OH-vah). Egg cells in the female. Plural of ovum. *See also* egg cell.

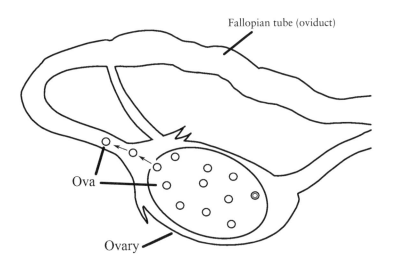

Fallopian tube (oviduct)

Ova

Ovary

**ovarian cyst** (oh-VAIR-ee-an sist). An abnormal growth on the ovary.

**ovarian follicles** (oh-VAIR-ee-an FALL-ick-els). Small spheres inside the ovaries, each containing one ovum.

**ovaries** (OH-vah-reez). Plural of ovary.

**ovary** (OH-vah-ree). The organ in the female where egg cells and sex hormones are produced and stored.

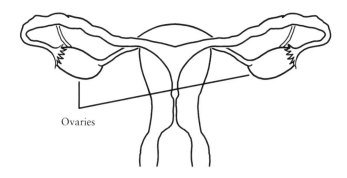

Ovaries

**oviducts** (OH-vah-ducts). *See* Fallopian tubes.

**ovulation** (ahv-you-LAY-shun). The release of an egg cell from the ovary, which occurs in a female about once a month. Ovulation may begin as early as age eight. The egg cell travels through the Fallopian tube to the uterus. There it is either fertilized by a sperm cell or expelled through menstruation.

O

Ovulation

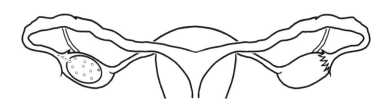

**ovulation method** (ahv-you-LAY-shun method). A type of fertility awareness method in which a female examines her vaginal discharge of cervical mucus to determine whether she is ovulating. *See also* fertility awareness method.

**ovum** (OH-vum). *See* egg cell.

**pad.** A narrow cotton pad that is placed in a female's undergarment to absorb blood during menstruation. Most are made with an adhesive on one side so that they will stick inside a woman's or girl's panties. Also called a sanitary napkin.

**Pap test** or **Pap smear.** A routine test performed in a doctor's office to test for cancer of the cervix.

**paracervical block** (para-SERV-ick-al block). A local anesthetic injected near the cervix (or neck of the uterus) to reduce pain during labor.

**parenting.** The skills used by a mother and father in bearing and rearing children.

**parturition** (par-chur-IH-shun). The action or process of giving birth to offspring. *See also* labor.

**passion** (PASH-un). An extremely strong emotion. The word can refer to love as well as anger.

**patch, the.** *See* contraceptive patch.

**paternal** (pa-TER-nal). Having to do with a father.

**pearly penile papules** (PER-lee PEE-nile PAP-yules). Small, dome-shaped bumps around the corona of the penis. The cause of this condition, which is harmless and does not need treatment, is unknown. When the bumps appear during puberty or adolescence, they often disappear over time.

P

**peer pressure.** When a person or group encourages a person of the same age to do something—such as have sex, take drugs, or drink alcohol—that the person doesn't want to do or that could get the person into trouble. This term commonly refers to young people in their preteen and teenage years.

**pelvic exam** (PEL-vik exam). A doctor's examination of a female's reproductive system to determine whether any health problems, such as cancer, sexually transmitted diseases, or infections, are present. It is usually performed by a primary care physician or gynecologist.

**pelvic inflammatory disease** (PEL-vik in-FLAM-ah-tory disease) or **PID.** A bacteria-caused infection that travels from the vagina or cervix to the uterus and Fallopian tubes. It can cause infertility.

**pelvis** (PEL-vis). The basin-shaped structure in the middle of the body, formed by the hip bones on the sides, pubic bone in front, and tail bone in back.

**penetration** (pen-eh-TRAY-shun). When something is placed inside a body opening during sexual activity. Although this term often refers to a penis entering the vagina, it can be used to describe other body openings (the mouth, the anus) and other body parts or even objects.

**penis** (PEE-nuhs). The major male sex organ. *See also* sex organs.

**penis shaft** (PEE-nuhs shaft). The main length of the penis, which is made up of erectile tissue covered by skin.

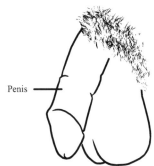

Penis

**performance anxiety** (per-FOR-mints ANG-zy-a-tee). A male's fear that he will not be able to achieve an erection during a sexual encounter. The fear sometimes prevents an erection.

**perinatal** (pair-ih-NAY-tuhl). Pertaining to or occurring during the period shortly before or shortly after birth.

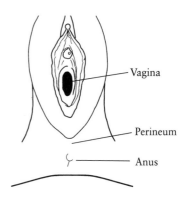

**perineum** (pare-eh-NEE-em). Usually refers to the area of the female anatomy located between the vagina and the anus. Also refers to the area of the male anatomy located between the scrotum and the anus.

**period.** *See* menstrual period.

**perspiration** (purr-spur-AY-shun). Liquid that is expelled from your skin cells to help keep you cool. You may perspire, or sweat, when you are hot or excited in some way.

**pervert** (PUR-vert). A person who commits unnatural sexual acts.

**petting.** *See* making out.

**physical traits.** Characteristics in a person's appearance that are inherited from his or her parents, such as eye color, hair color, height, and weight.

**pill, the.** *See* birth control pills.

**pimples** (PIM-puhlz). *See* acne.

**pituitary gland** (pih-TOO-ah-tair-ee gland). A tiny gland at the base of the brain that controls the other glands in the body. During adolescence, it begins the process of changing a girl into a young woman and a boy into a young man.

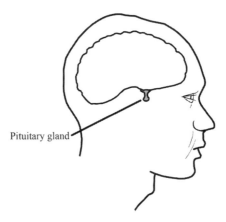

Pituitary gland

**placenta** (pluh-CENT-ah). A temporary, waffle-shaped organ that exchanges nutrients and wastes between the mother and the fetus. The placenta also produces hormones necessary to maintain pregnancy. The placenta leaves the body after the baby is born, and is then called the afterbirth.

P

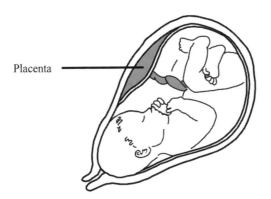

Placenta

**PMS.** *See* premenstrual syndrome.

**polygamy** (pah-LIG-ah-me). Marriage in which the male has more than one wife or the female may have more than one husband.

**pornography** (por-NAH-gra-fee). Books, magazines, videos, and other material that show or describe erotic activities for the purpose of sexual excitement.

**postpartum** (post-PAR-tum). The time following the birth of a child.

**postpartum depression** (post-PAR-tum depression). A period of sadness and unhappiness some women experience after the birth of a child. It is believed to be caused mostly by sudden hormonal changes that happen in a woman's body after she gives birth. Stress, lack of sleep, and other factors may also add to depression. Postpartum depression can happen right after a baby is born, or even weeks later. New mothers who feel depressed should talk to their doctors; there are ways to help ease the depression. Also referred to as baby blues.

**preeclampsia** (PRE-uh-CLAMP-see-uh). A serious condition a woman can develop during pregnancy in which she has high blood pressure, severe edema (swelling), and protein in her urine. It can result in the death of the mother or fetus if not controlled. Also called pregnancy-induced hypertension or toxemia.

**pre-ejaculatory fluid** (pre-ee-JACK-yuh-la-tor-ee FLU-id). Mucus produced by the Cowper's glands before a male ejaculates. It serves to lubricate the end of the penis before intercourse and to protect sperm as it passes through the male's urethra.

**preemie.** *See* premature baby.

**pregnancy.** The nine-month period (actually, 40 weeks) following conception when a baby develops inside its mother's uterus.

**pregnancy-induced hypertension.** *See* preeclampsia.

**Pregnant**

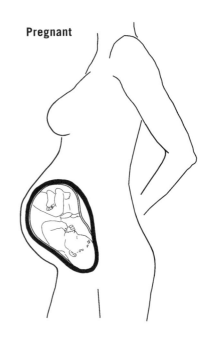

**pregnant.** Refers to a woman who is carrying an unborn child inside her uterus.

**premarital intercourse** (pree-MARE-it-al IN-ter-kors) or **pre-marital sex** (pree-MARE-it-al seks). Having sexual relations before marriage.

**premature baby.** A baby born before the full forty weeks of the mother's pregnancy, usually weighing under five pounds.

**premenstrual syndrome** (PREE-men-stroo-al sin-drome) or **PMS.** When a woman or girl has unpleasant symptoms a few days before her monthly menstrual period begins, including headaches, bloating, cramps, and irritability.

**prenatal** (pre-NAY-tuhl). The time or period before birth.

**prenatal care** (pre-NAY-tuhl care). The health care given to a mother during her pregnancy.

**prepuce** (PRE-pyoos). Can refer either to the foreskin of a male's penis or a similar fold of skin covering a female's clitoris. On the female, it is also referred to as the clitoral hood.

**prescription drugs.** Medications that are available only with a doctor's or nurse practitoner's prescription. Prescription drugs can be dangerous if they are used in ways different from how they are prescribed, or by people who did not get the prescription.

**preventive behavior.** Behavior that gives at least some protection against spreading sexually transmitted diseases.

**pro-choice.** The belief that a pregnant woman should have the right to choose whether to continue the pregnancy or to end it.

**progesterone** (pro-JESS-ter-ohn). The female sex hormone, which prepares a woman's uterus to receive and sustain a fertilized egg. It is sometimes called the "pregnancy hormone." It also causes a mother's breasts to produce milk for a newborn baby.

**prolapsed cord** (PRO-lapst cord). An umbilical cord that has wrapped around the unborn baby's neck and restricted blood flow to the baby. This endangers the baby's life during childbirth and may require a doctor to deliver the baby by Cesarean section.

**pro-life.** The belief that abortion should be illegal because it is the taking of human life.

P

**promiscuous** (pro-MIS-cue-us). Behavior in which a person randomly and casually engages in sexual activity, usually with several different partners in a short period of time.

**prostaglandin** (PRAHS-tuh-GLAN-dun). A chemical the female body releases when the uterus sheds its lining each month during the menstrual period. It causes the uterus to contract, which is the reason some women experience cramping.

**prostate gland** (PRAH-state gland). A gland surrounding the male urethra. From it comes a milky fluid that is part of the semen. The muscles around the urethra are the main source of ejaculation.

**prostatitis** (pros-tah-TITE-us). Inflammation of the prostate.

**puberty** (PYOO-ber-tee). The years between approximately ages ten and thirteen, when girls begin to change into young women and boys begin to change into young men. These changes happen at different times for every boy and girl. *See also* adolescence.

**pubic hair** (PYOO-bic hair). Hair surrounding the sexual organs of a girl or a boy. This hair develops during adolescence.

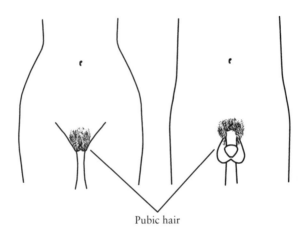

Pubic hair

**pubic lice.** *See* crab lice.

**pudendum** (pyoo-DEN-dum). The external sexual organs of a human being, especially of a woman.

**pullout method.** *See* coitus interruptus.

**purge.** In terms of eating or diet, the word "purge" means to force yourself to vomit in order to get rid of what you've just eaten. Some adolescents get into a binge-and-purge cycle, where they eat large amounts of food quickly, then deliberately vomit it.

**quickening.** The time during a mother's pregnancy when she first begins to feel the movement of the baby in the uterus. It usually occurs about the fourth or fifth month.

**rape.** Being forced to have sexual intercourse without your consent. Rape may be by physical force, but any sexual act that you have not agreed to also may be rape.

**raphe** (RAY-fee). A continuous ridge of tissue that creates a line. It is found in different parts of the body, including one on the male reproductive organs, which extends from the anus through the middle of the scrotum and along the middle of the underside of the penis.

**recessive trait** (re-SESS-iv trait). An inherited trait that is not dominant, but is overridden by another inherited trait. For example, brown eyes are dominant and blue eyes are recessive, meaning that if one parent contributes a gene for brown eyes and the other parent contributes a gene for blue eyes, the baby will have brown eyes. *See also* dominant trait.

**reproduction** (ree-pro-DUK-shun). The process of having children or "reproducing" human life.

Q
R

**reproductive organs** (ree-pro-DUK-tiv OR-gunz). The organs in the body of a male or female that have to do with producing children, including the penis and the uterus. *See also* sex organs.

**retractile testicles** (ree-TRACK-tuhl TES-tic-uhlz). A condition in which one or both of a young boy's testicles pulls up to the top of the scrotum or into the body from time to time. It usually corrects itself by the time the boy reaches puberty. If it doesn't, it may need to be surgically corrected.

**Rh incompatibility** (R-H in-come-pat-ih-BIL-it-ee). This happens when a mother has Rh-negative blood and her baby has Rh-positive blood, or vice versa. The mother's blood produces antibodies that may endanger the fetuses of future pregnancies. Injections of gamma globulin are given to the mother to prevent her body from producing these antibodies.

**rhythm method** (RIH-them method). *See* calendar method.

**risky behavior.** Behavior that may lead to a sexually transmitted disease such as HIV/AIDS.

**romance** (ro-MANS). Love or passion.

**romantic love.** An intimate or passionate love.

**rubber.** *See* condom.

R

**saddle block.** A type of anesthesia given by injection into the mother's lower spinal area to block pain during labor and delivery.

**safe behavior.** Behavior that prevents sexually transmitted diseases.

**safe sex** or **safer sex.** Sexual activity that is unlikely to expose a person to HIV or other sexually transmitted diseases because no body fluids are shared (other than saliva). Examples include using a condom during intercourse and engaging only in outercourse.

**sanitary napkin.** *See* pad.

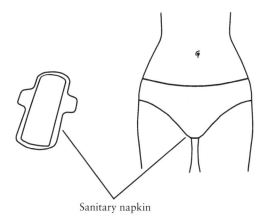

Sanitary napkin

S

**scrotum** (SKRO-tum). The sac under the penis containing the testicles.

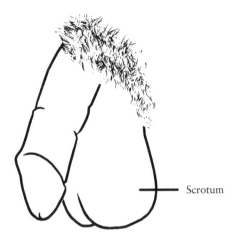

Scrotum

**sebaceous glands** (see-BAY-shus glandz). Glands that secrete an oily material under the skin. These glands are particularly active during adolescence.

**sebum** (SEE-bem). Fatty lubricant secreted by the sebaceous glands of the skin. Sometimes associated with acne.

**secondary sexual characteristics** (SEC-un-dare-ee SEKS-you-uhl CARE-ick-ter-IS-ticks). The changes that occur in a young person's body during adolescence, such as the development of hair under the arms, pubic hair, a deepening voice in boys, and breasts in girls.

**seed.** Sometimes refers to sperm cells. *See* sperm.

**self-control.** In a sexual sense, acting responsibly and not giving in to impulsive actions. *See also* safe behavior.

S

**semen** (SEE-mun). Thick, white fluid that contains sperm and is ejaculated from the penis.

**seminal vesicles** (SEM-in-al VESS-ick-als). Two sacs where semen is stored. They are located near the prostate gland.

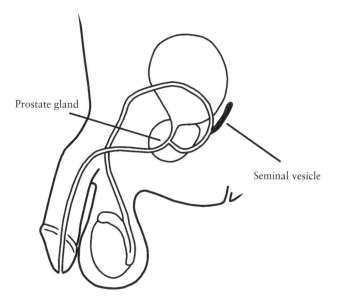

Prostate gland

Seminal vesicle

**seminiferous tubules** (sem-in-IF-er-us TU-byuls). Structures in the testes that produce sperm.

**sex** (seks). Male or female. Also refers to sexual intercourse. *See also* gender; intercourse.

**sex organs** (seks OR-gunz). The organs that are part of the reproductive system. The major sex organ for a male is his penis; for a female, it is her vagina. *See also* reproductive organs.

# Female Sex Organs

**Internal view**

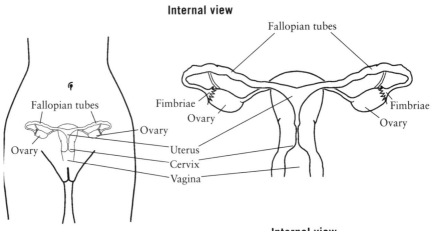

Fallopian tubes

Fallopian tubes

Fimbriae

Ovary

Ovary

Fimbriae

Ovary

Ovary

Uterus

Cervix

Vagina

**Internal view**

**External view**

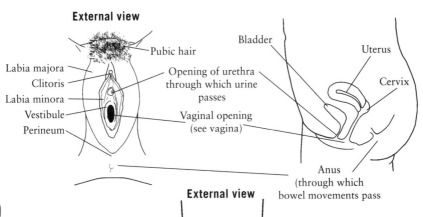

Pubic hair

Bladder

Uterus

Labia majora

Clitoris

Labia minora

Vestibule

Perineum

Opening of urethra
through which urine
passes

Vaginal opening
(see vagina)

Cervix

Anus
(through which
bowel movements pass

**External view**

## Male Sex Organs

**Internal view**

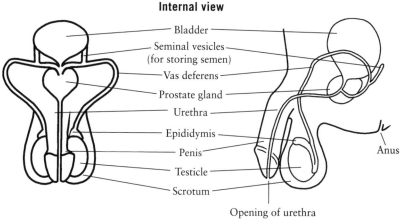

Bladder
Seminal vesicles
(for storing semen)
Vas deferens
Prostate gland
Urethra
Epididymis
Penis
Testicle
Scrotum
Anus

Opening of urethra
through which urine
and semen pass

**External view**

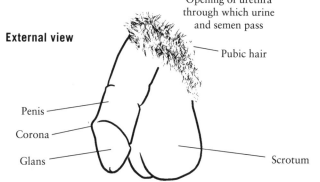

Pubic hair

Penis
Corona
Glans
Scrotum

**External view**

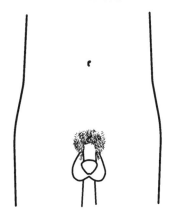

**sex role** (seks role). The way a society establishes how a man or woman ought to behave. Also refers to what is expected of a mother or father.

**sexual characteristics** (SEK-shoo-uhl CARE-ick-ter-IS-ticks). Those characteristics that distinguish a man from a woman, including the sex organs, breasts, facial hair, and the Adam's apple. *See also* secondary sexual characteristics.

**sexual intercourse** (SEK-shoo-uhl IN-ter-kors). *See* intercourse.

**sexual intimacy** (SEK-shoo-uhl IN-tih-muh-see). The expression of physical feeling through sexual behavior.

**sexual orientation** (SEK-shoo-uhl OR-ee-en-TAY-shun). Refers to a person's sexual preference in terms of whether he or she is bisexual (attracted to both sexes), heterosexual (attracted to people of the opposite sex), or homosexual (attracted to people of the same sex).

**sexuality** (SEK-shoo-AL-uh-tee). A person's sexual nature; having to do with being male or female. Also refers to sexual behavior.

**sexually active** (SEK-shoo-uhl-ee active). Usually used to mean someone who is having intimate sexual relations with another, or with more than one other person.

**sexually transmitted diseases** (SEK-shoo-uhl-ee transmitted diseases) **(STDs)**. Diseases that may result from sexual intercourse or other intimate contact. Also called venereal diseases.

**sexy.** Sexually attractive or interesting.

**shield, the.** A barrier method of contraception in which a soft silicone cup fits snugly over the cervix to block sperm from entering. It is used with spermicide to prevent pregnancy.

**Siamese twins** (SIE-uh-MEEZ twinz). *See* conjoined twins.

**Skene's glands** (skeens glandz). Two small glands located in the vagina near the lower end of the urethra. Some experts believe that the glands produce a fluid that is ejaculated during a woman's orgasm.

**smegma** (SMEG-mah). A thick, white substance that collects under the foreskin of a uncircumcised male, if the foreskin is not pulled back and cleaned. This substance can cause odor and irritation. It also can collect under the foreskin of a girl's clitoris. These areas need to be cleaned daily with soap and water.

**sodomy** (SAW-duh-mee). The act of having anal or oral intercourse, or intercourse with an animal. The word comes from the biblical story of Sodom.

**speculum** (SPEK-you-lum). A medical instrument used to hold open the walls of the vagina during a pelvic exam and Pap smear.

**sperm** or **sperm cell.** The male reproductive cell. When a sperm cell meets with an egg cell in the female's body during intercourse, a baby may be conceived.

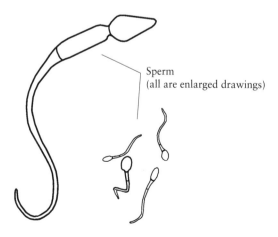

Sperm
(all are enlarged drawings)

S

**spermatozoa** (sper-MA-tah-ZOE-uh). The scientific name for sperm cells.

**spermicide** (SPER-ma-side). A substance that kills sperm cells and is used to help prevent pregnancy.

**spirochetes** (SPY-ro-keets). Slender corkscrew-shaped bacteria that cause syphilis.

**spontaneous erection** (spontaneous ee-RECK-shun). When a male gets an erection without having any sexual feelings or thoughts. This often happens to boys during puberty because of the hormonal increases their bodies are experiencing.

**spotting.** Small amounts of vaginal bleeding that may occur between a female's menstrual periods. This is a common side-effect of many types of contraceptives that use hormones.

**spouse.** A marriage partner, either male or female.

**statutory rape.** A criminal act that happens when an adult has sex with a minor, even if the minor agreed to engage in sex. Under the law, a minor is not considered to be capable of making a responsible decision regarding whether to have sex.

**sterility** (ster-ILL-eh-tee). Being sterile or unable to have children.

**sterilization** (stare-ill-ih-ZAY-shun). A surgical procedure that prevents a man from impregnating a woman or a woman from becoming pregnant.

**stillbirth.** When a fetus that has died in the mother's womb, or during labor or delivery, is expelled or removed from the woman's body.

**straight.** *See* heterosexual.

**stretch marks.** Lines that can appear when a part of the body, such as a female's breasts, grows. Women may also experience stretch marks on the abdomen as a result of pregnancy.

**sweat glands** (swet glandz). Glands, particularly under the arms, that become more active during adolescence. Greater body odor is normal as a young person matures, and greater effort is needed to keep the body clean.

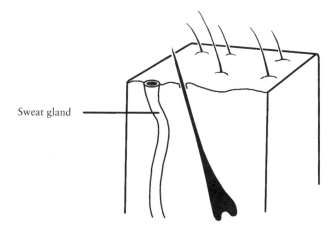

Sweat gland

**sympathetic pregnancy.** *See* couvade syndrome.

**syphilis** (SIH-fill-iss). A serious but curable sexually transmitted disease.

S

**tampon** (TAM-pahn). A small roll of absorbent cotton a female inserts into her vagina to absorb menstrual flow.

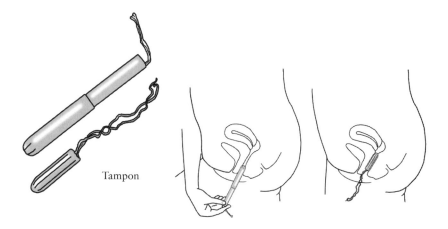

Tampon

**T-cells.** Another name for T-lymphocytes, also known as white blood cells. HIV, the virus that causes AIDS, destroys these cells. A healthy person has one thousand to two thousand T-cells per cubic millimeter of blood. A person who has HIV is considered to have AIDS when his or her T-cells are down to about two hundred per cubic millimeter of blood.

T

**temperature method.** A fertility awareness method of birth control in which the female takes her basal body temperature each day to determine whether she is ovulating and so is more fertile. She tries to avoid pregnancy by not having intercourse when she is likely to be most fertile, or to increase the chance of becoming pregnant by having intercourse when she is most fertile. *See also* fertility awareness method.

**teratogen** (teh-RAT-eh-jen). Any agent that might interfere with the normal development of a fetus and result in the loss of a pregnancy, a birth defect, or a pregnancy complication. Teratogens can be in the form of medication, alcohol, cigarettes, infectious diseases, chemicals in the environment, or other agents.

**test tube baby.** A baby conceived by in vitro fertilization.

**testes** (TES-teez) or **testicles** (TES-tic-uhlz). Two oval-shaped glands that produce sperm cells. They are located inside the scrotum.

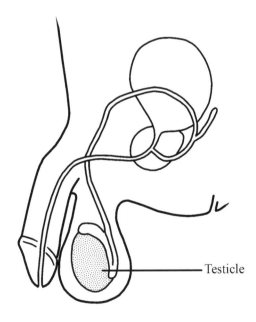

Testicle

**testicular self-examination** (tes-TIC-u-lar self-examination) or **TSE.** A technique for examining the testicles for lumps or other abnormalities in order to find testicular cancer in its earliest stages, when it is more likely to be successfully treated.

**testosterone** (tes-TOSS-ter-ohn). A hormone, produced in the testicles, that affects the development of male sexual characteristics. Production of the hormone increases during puberty, resulting in growth of muscles, facial and body hair, sperm production, and other changes.

**tongue kiss.** *See* French kiss.

**toxemia** (tocks-EE-me-uh). *See* preeclampsia.

**toxic shock syndrome** or **TSS.** A rare condition affecting both males and females, caused by staph bacteria. Females who use tampons have a slight risk of contracting TSS. If tampons are not changed frequently enough, it allows the bacteria in the blood to multiply, leading to the condition. Symptoms include fever, vomiting, and diarrhea; the condition can be fatal.

**transgender** (TRANZ-JEN-der). A person who feels he or she is the opposite sex, or who does not identify with either sex, female or male.

**transmission** (trans-MIH-shun). The process of transmitting or passing along. In the context of disease, transmission refers to passing something from one person to another.

T

**trichomoniasis** (trik-oh-moe-NYE-uh-sis). A common sexually transmitted disease. It mostly affects women. Symptoms include a foul-smelling or frothy green discharge from the vagina, vaginal itching or redness, pain during sexual intercourse, lower abdominal discomfort, and the urge to urinate. Men usually have no symptoms, but when symptoms are present, they include discharge from the urethra, the urge to urinate, and a burning sensation with urination.

**trimester** (try-MESS-ter). A three-month period of time. The nine months of a woman's pregnancy are divided into the first, second, and third trimesters.

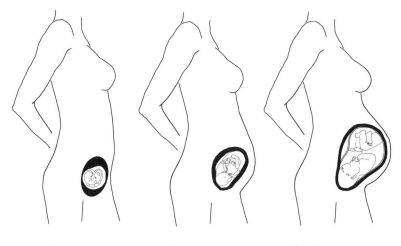

First trimester          Second trimester          Third trimester

**tubal ligation** (TOO-buhl lye-GAY-shun). A surgical procedure used to block a woman's Fallopian tubes to prevent pregnancy. Commonly referred to as "getting the tubes tied."

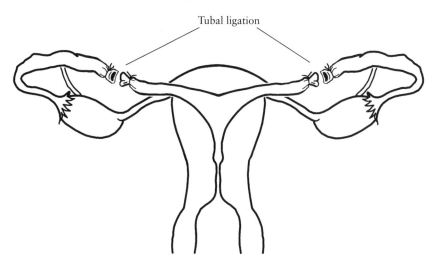

Tubal ligation

**tubal pregnancy** (TOO-buhl pregnancy). A serious condition that occurs when a fertilized egg begins to develop in a mother's Fallopian tube instead of inside the uterus. *See also* ectopic pregnancy.

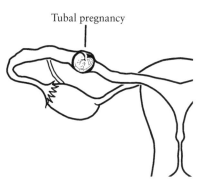

Tubal pregnancy

T

**twins.** Two offspring resulting from one pregnancy. *See also* fraternal twins; identical twins.

**U**

**ultrasound** (ULL-truh-sound). Vibrations of the same physical nature as sound, but at frequencies above the range of human hearing. Similar to an X-ray, the ultrasound has many uses, one of which is to look at a growing fetus in the womb to monitor its health and growth. It can also show the sex of the fetus and help determine when it will be born.

**umbilical cord** (um-BILL-ick-uhl cord). The cord that attaches an unborn baby to its mother's uterus. Through the cord, the embryo receives nourishment from the mother. *See also* navel.

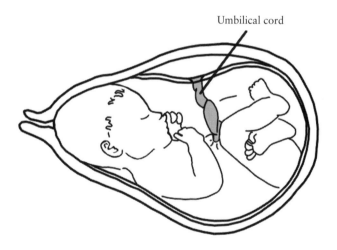

Umbilical cord

**undescended testicles.** A condition in which one or both of a male's testicles remain inside the body, rather than descending into the scrotum as normal. If the testicles do not descend in the first year of a boy's life, he should have an operation to bring them into the scrotum. Otherwise, the testicles may not develop properly and could develop cancer.

**ureter** (you-REE-ter). A duct that carries urine from the kidney to the bladder.

**urethra** (you-REE-thra). The tube through which urine passes from the bladder during urination. In a male, sperm also is ejaculated through the urethra.

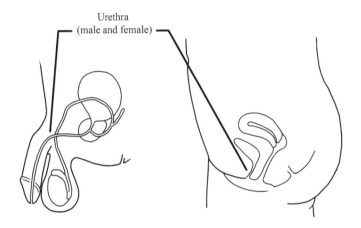

Urethra
(male and female)

**urinary opening** (UR-ih-ner-ee opening). The small opening at the end of the urethra where urine comes out. In the male, semen also comes out of this opening.

**urinary tract infection** (UR-ih-ner-ee trackt infection) or **UTI.** An infection of the urinary tract that causes painful urination.

**urinate** (UR-ih-nate). To expel urine from the body. Urine contains waste from blood that has been processed by the kidneys.

**uterine contractions** (YOU-ter-uhn con-TRACK-shuns). *See* contractions.

**uterine lining** (YOU-ter-uhn lining). *See* endometrium.

**uterus** (YOU-ter-us). The hollow organ in which a fertilized egg cell develops into a baby. Also called the womb.

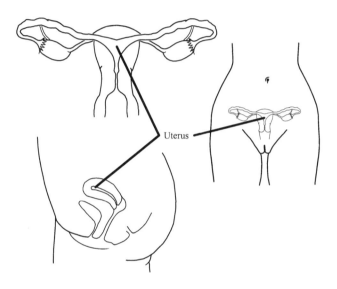

Uterus

**vagina** (va-JYE-nah). The female's major sex organ, it is a passageway leading from the uterus to the outside of a woman's body. The man's penis is inserted into the vagina during intercourse, and a baby is normally born through the vagina. *See also* sex organs.

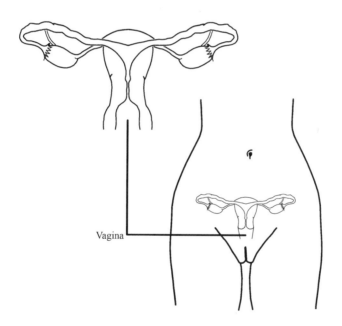

Vagina

**vaginal fluids** (VAH-jin-uhl fluids). Fluids produced in the vagina.

**vaginal intercourse** (VAH-jin-uhl IN-ter-kors). *See* intercourse.

**vaginitis** (vah-jin-ITE-is). Inflammation of the vagina, often accompanied by irritation and infection.

V

**varicocele** (VAR-uh-koe-seel). An abnormal enlargement of the veins in the scrotum. The condition can cause pain and, in some cases, infertility. Pain can be lessened with medication, a scrotal support, or both. The condition can be surgically corrected.

**vas deferens** (vas DEF-er-enz). One of a pair of tubes through which sperm cells pass from the testicles.

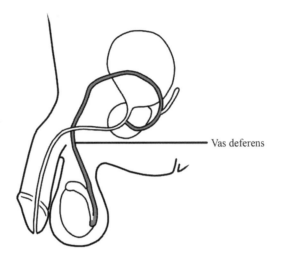

Vas deferens

**vasectomy** (vas-ECK-tuh-mee). A surgical procedure on a male that prevents sperm from moving through the vas deferens. This is a method of sterilization to prevent pregnancy.

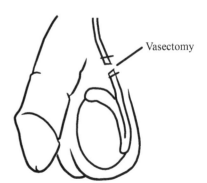

Vasectomy

**venereal disease** (vuh-NEER-ee-uhl disease) or **VD.** *See* sexually transmitted diseases.

V

**vestibule** (VES-teh-bule). In a female, the space between the labia minora into which the vagina and urethra open.

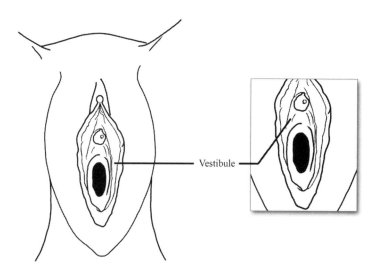

Vestibule

**viable** (VI-uh-bul). Able to live and develop normally. Usually refers to a baby that is able to live and grow outside the uterus.

**virgin** (VUR-jun). A person who has not had sexual intercourse.

**virtuous** (VIR-choo-us). Conforming to high principles. Often refers to being chaste or not having sexual intercourse before marriage.

**vulva** (VULL-vah). The female's external sex organs. The vulva includes the mons veneris, labia, clitoris, and vaginal opening.

V

**wet dream.** *See* nocturnal emission.

**wife.** The female partner in a marriage.

**withdrawal.** *See* coitus interruptus.

**womb** (woom). *See* uterus.

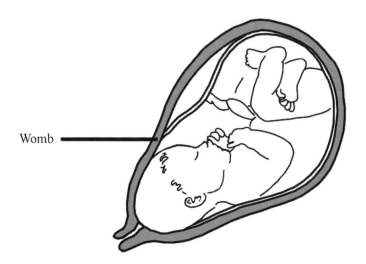

Womb

**yeast infection** (yeest infection). An infection that causes itching and burning in the vagina.

**zits.** *See* acne.

**zygote** (ZI-gote). A fertilized ovum (egg cell). This is the first stage in the development of a baby inside the mother's body. Three to four days after fertilization, the zygote develops into a morula.

Y
Z

# Games and Puzzles

## Ten Letters

Cross out 10 of the letters below and what do you have left?
(Clue: The word has to do with having a baby.)

P A Z L T E A K M B S Z O B R

## Twenty Letters

Cross out 20 of the letters below and what do you have left?
(Clue: A baby normally travels through this.)

T E B C K I R R A T F H K M P Q Z C O R A P B R N M C A E L

# All the Same #1

Find another word for each of the following. (Hint: Each of the five answers begins with the same letter of the alphabet.)

women's breasts _____

hymen _____

boy or man _____

motherly _____

legal union of two people _____

# All the Same #2

Find another word for each of the following. (Hint: Each of the five answers begins with the same letter of the alphabet.)

pimples _____

acquired immunodeficiency syndrome _____

removal of an unborn fetus _____

when a girl changes into a young woman
and a boy changes into a young man _____

part of the body where the stomach,
intestines, and, in a woman, the uterus are _____

## Word Search

Find eight words dealing with growing up and dating.

```
P A N G R O M X E O R I V E L

E P I M P L E S H L A K U M A

L O U D H E T A F I C A I O P

V I R B A L K G L A N H I T E

A D O L E S C E N C E L F I T

X A V E P R A I G E U E A O K

G L O Z Z I T S H D A T I N G

K I S S A P E Y U N G I L S T
```

ANSWERS:

# Know Your Words

Circle the correct letter

1. An unborn baby is called a:
   a. fimbria
   b. sebum
   c. fetus

2. A doctor who delivers babies is:
   a. an obstetrician
   b. a vasectomy
   c. a heterosexual

3. An IUD is:
   a. a newborn baby
   b. the menstrual cycle
   c. a birth control device

4. Not being able to get pregnant means being:
   a. infertile
   b. nauseated
   c. bisexual

5. A baby born before nine months is a:
   a. Lamaze baby
   b. premature baby
   c. Wasserman baby

6. Breastfeeding is also called:
   a. nursing
   b. copulation
   c. necking

7. Fontanel is another name for a baby's:
   a. bladder
   b. "soft spot"
   c. abdomen

8. Puberty is another name for:
   a. adolescence
   b. quickening
   c. AIDS

9. An operation that prevents a person from having children is:
   a. zygote
   b. sterilization
   c. syphilis

10. This is removed during circumcision:
    a. Adam's apple
    b. nipple
    c. foreskin

11. A female homosexual is a:
    a. gynecologist
    b. lesbian
    c. virgin

12. When a sperm cell and an egg cell join, it's the moment of:
    a. abstinence
    b. conception
    c. birth control

13. Coitus is:
    a. sexual intercourse
    b. an emotion
    c. part of the abdomen

14. Fertile:
    a. change of life
    b. able to conceive
    c. bosom

15. Gender is:
    a. amniocentesis
    b. being male or female
    c. basal body temperature method

16. Herpes is:
    a. a flu germ
    b. a growth spurt
    c. a viral disease of the skin

17. A person who is attracted to someone of the same sex:
    a. mate
    b. midwife
    c. homosexual

18. It's also called "change of life":
    a. abstinence
    b. sex change
    c. menopause

19. Hormones are:
    a. urinary tract infections
    b. chemicals secreted by the glands
    c. membranes in the body

20. The release of an egg cell from the ovary is:
    a. ovulation
    b. endometrium
    c. gestation

ANSWERS: 1. C. FETUS, 2. A. OBSTETRICIAN, 3. C. A BIRTH CONTROL DEVICE, 4. A. INFERTILE, 5. B. PREMATURE BABY, 6. A. NURSING, 7. B. "SOFT SPOT," 8. A. ADOLESCENCE, 9. B. STERILIZATION, 10. C. FORESKIN, 11. B. LESBIAN, 12. B. CONCEPTION, 13. A. SEXUAL INTERCOURSE, 14. B. ABLE TO CONCEIVE, 15. B. BEING MALE OR FEMALE, 16. C. A VIRAL DISEASE OF THE SKIN, 17. C. HOMOSEXUAL, 18. C. MENOPAUSE, 19. B. CHEMICALS SECRETED BY THE GLANDS, 20. A. OVULATION

# Crossword Puzzle

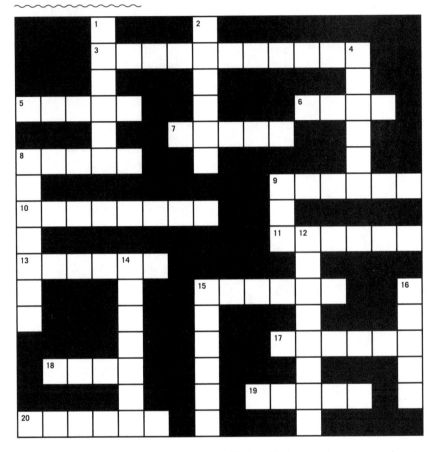

**Across**

3. Time period when a girl changes into a woman and a boy into a man
5. Part of the body between the top of the legs and the abdomen
6. Human being right after birth
7. Spot where the umbilical cord was connected to the abdomen
8. Forcing yourself to vomit what you've just eaten
9. A fertilized egg cell
10. Enlargement and hardening of a penis
11. Glands that make sperm cells
13. Duct that carries urine from the kidney to the bladder
15. Male contraceptive device
17. Bumps on a man's chest and at the tip of a woman's breasts

18. Sexual intercourse when one person doesn't want to participate
19. Units of heredity carried by the chromosomes
20. White blood cells

**Down**

1. When two people spend time together in a romantic relationship
2. Having to do with male or female characteristics or activities
4. The fourth stage of development of a new human being
8. Foreskin or clitoral hood
9. Pimple
12. Feelings
14. Ovum
15. The opening or neck of the uterus
16. Very fat